Sandra Day O'Connor

■

SUPREME COURT JUSTICE

Lisa McElroy

A Gateway Biography

The Millbrook Press
Brookfield, Connecticut

*For Sandra Day O'Connor, who was sworn into the
Supreme Court the month I began high school, and who made
me believe, then and now, that I could achieve anything.
Many thanks for your courtesy and kindness.*

*Special thanks to Veronica Amaral, Francesca Suppa,
Jill Grochmal, and the O'Connor family for their assistance with
this book. Thanks also to Steve, Zoe, and Abby for their
continual love and support.*

Published by The Millbrook Press, Inc.
2 Old New Milford Road
Brookfield, CT 06804

Library of Congress Cataloging-in-Publication Data
McElroy, Lisa Tucker.
Sandra Day O'Connor : Supreme Court justice / Lisa McElroy.
p. cm. — (A Gateway biography)
Summary: A biography of Sandra Day O'Connor who, in 1981, became the first
woman appointed as Supreme Court justice.
Includes bibliographical references and index.
ISBN 0-7613-2502-6 (lib. bdg.)
1. O'Connor, Sandra Day, 1930—Juvenile literature. 2. Judges—United
States—Biography—Juvenile literature. 3. United States. Supreme Court—
Biography—Juvenile literature. [1. O'Connor, Sandra Day, 1930- 2. Judges.
3. United States. Supreme Court—Biography. 4. Women—Biography.]
I. Title. II. Series.
KF8745.O25M386 2003   347.73'2634—dc21   2003002230

Cover photograph courtesy of AP/Wide World Photos
Photographs courtesy of Getty Images: pp. 1 (Liaison), 27 (Hulton/Archive), 39
(© Karin Cooper/Liaison), 42-43 (©Reuters/William Collins); Collection of the
Supreme Court of the United States: pp. 4 (photograph by Michael Evans, The
White House), 33 (photographs by Franz Jantzen); © Jay Mallin: pp. 6, 8, 11
(both), 13, 15, 18, 20; © Bettmann/Corbis: p. 25; AP/Wide World Photos: pp.
28, 30-31, 36, 40

Sandra Day O'Connor

Associate Justice Sandra Day O'Connor is sworn in by Chief Justice Warren Burger while her husband, John O'Connor, holds the Bible.

I, Sandra Day O'Connor, do solemnly swear that I will administer justice without respect to persons and do equal right to the poor and to the rich, and that I will faithfully and impartially discharge and perform all of the duties incumbent upon me as an Associate Justice of the United States Supreme Court under the Constitution and laws of the United States. So help me God.

With tears in her eyes, Sandra Day O'Connor spoke this oath before a courtroom packed with people, and then put on her black robes. She walked to the end of the bench, where eight men in their own black robes sat. There was an empty seat waiting for her. In the front row of the thousands of people watching, her parents, husband, and three sons looked on with pride. President Ronald Reagan grinned. When this happy ceremony took place, on September 25, 1981, Sandra Day O'Connor became the first woman to serve on the United States Supreme Court.

It was a day that she and many others had thought would never come. Sandra thought of herself as a cowgirl, mother, and lawyer from Arizona. To feminists and politicians across the country, however, she was much more. To them, a woman on the Supreme Court meant that women were being accepted as equal, contributing members of American society. Sandra became a symbol of what women from all walks of life had long been fighting for: leadership, opportunity, and professional challenges for women.

Sandra Day was born on March 26, 1930, in El Paso, Texas. She was the oldest child of Harry and Ada Mae Day, who owned the Lazy B, a very large ranch in southeastern Arizona. Young Sandra enjoyed ranch life. She loved to ride her horse, Chico, do ranch chores, and hang out with the cowboys.

The Lazy B ranch in Arizona where Sandra lived as a child

First, But Not Last

Many people have written about Sandra Day O'Connor being the first woman on the United States Supreme Court. To Justice O'Connor, however, the most important thing has been to make sure that she would not be the last. Justice O'Connor is very aware of the role she plays in history. When Ronald Reagan chose her to be a justice in 1981, O'Connor realized that everyone in the whole country would be watching to see whether she did a good job as a Supreme Court justice. She said at the time, "I think the important thing about my appointment is not that I will decide cases as a woman, but that I am a woman who will get to decide cases."

Justice O'Connor worked very hard at being a good justice from her very first day in office. Says O'Connor, "It seems to me . . . that a wise old woman and a wise old man will reach the same decision and I think that's generally true." She is now recognized as one of the most influential and respected justices on the court. She is also especially happy to have a female colleague on the court, Justice Ruth Bader Ginsburg, who was appointed by Bill Clinton in 1993.

Sandra became an excellent horseback rider, and still loves to ride.

Sandra also took pleasure in working on the ranch with her parents. Because she was involved in the family business of ranching from a very early age, she felt that she understood her parents and their jobs much better than other children did. She has said, "How many young people see their father leave for the office but don't really know what he does for a living?" Sandra did know what her father did, because she watched him and helped on the ranch every day.

While it was fun and exciting for Sandra to grow up on the Lazy B, the ranch could also be a lonely place. Because she was an only child for eight years, the cowboys and the farm animals became her playmates, baby-sitters, and friends. Sandra also read books to help her learn about life outside the ranch. She has said, "Books were my best friends at the ranch. There was always time to read, and my parents kept a library." As a young girl, and as she grew older, Sandra's favorite books were an encyclopedia set called *The Book of Knowledge,* because in these books she could learn about so many things. She also read and enjoyed the Nancy Drew books, *Black Beauty*, and *The Wizard of Oz*, among many others.

The ranch was very isolated, and the nearest school was almost thirty miles away. Her parents wanted her to get the best possible education but did not want her to travel so far every day. When she was five years old, Sandra went to live with her grandmother, Mamie Scott Wilkey, in El Paso, Texas. There she was enrolled in the Radford School for Girls. At first, Sandra was homesick. She missed her parents and the ranch a lot. However, she soon made many friends, including Beverly Timberlake, whose father also had a ranch. Sandra's cousin Flournoy Davis became her very best friend.

Sandra loved school. She enjoyed learning and reading and was an excellent student. Although she tried

> As a child, Sandra Day O'Connor was afraid of rattlesnakes and insects, both of which were plentiful on the Arizona ranch.

hard to obey the rules and listen to her teachers, she didn't always succeed. One time, when she was in third or fourth grade, she swung a softball bat at a window and broke it. She was embarrassed to be called to the principal's office to explain.

Even though she did well at Radford, Sandra always missed the ranch a great deal. This was especially true when her sister, Ann, and her brother, Alan, were born in the late 1930s. For many years she could not wait to go home to the ranch every summer, and she often took her cousin Flournoy with her for company. When she was about eleven, she felt so homesick that she con-vinced her parents to let her move home to the ranch during the school year and go to school in Lordsburg, the nearest town to the Lazy B. Her parents reluctantly agreed, and Sandra began making the 30-mile (48-kilometer) trip from the ranch to school every day. Eventually, though, the long trip to school would prove to be too much, and after only one year Sandra and her parents saw that it would be better for her to return to El Paso and Radford.

When Justice O'Connor was a student at Radford, she met Eleanor Roosevelt. The justice says that she will always remember the First Lady's strong handshake.

Sandra (left) with her best friend and cousin, Flournoy, while visiting their horses on the ranch

Sandra poses for an Easter photo with her mother and little sister and brother in 1940.

Healthy Body, Healthy Mind

Justice O'Connor is a firm believer in physical fitness. As a child, she learned from the rigors of growing up on a ranch that it is important for everyone to be strong and healthy. Ever since she was in high school and learned to play tennis, Justice O'Connor has made a point of exercising every day.

Justice O'Connor loves to play golf and tennis. In fact, she is recognized as an excellent golfer and even shot a hole-in-one in 2001 at the age of seventy-one!

As soon as she joined the Supreme Court, Justice O'Connor began working out at the gym that is on the top floor of the court building. In fact, she even started an aerobics class there for the women at the court. The class takes place early in the morning, before court employees must report for work. Justice O'Connor says that the aerobics class makes her feel healthy and helps her think more clearly during her busy day that follows.

Because she was very smart, Sandra skipped a grade and graduated from Radford when she was only twelve. She went on to Austin High School in El Paso. There, she learned to play tennis, a sport she would enjoy all her life. She could not play on the tennis team, however, or any other team, because at the time there were no athletic teams for girls at her school.

She did join the Spanish Club, the Drama Club, and the student newspaper. She enjoyed being involved in school activities and made many friends.

Sandra also studied hard in the hope of attending Stanford, a California university. Her father had planned to attend Stanford when he was a young man. When his father died, Sandra's dad had to

A portrait of Sandra at age sixteen, when she was looking forward to attending Stanford University

quit school to work on the ranch. The counselors at her school warned Sandra not to hope too hard to be admitted. Stanford is a very hard school to get into, and Sandra was very young. But at age sixteen, Sandra was excited to learn that she would be part of the Stanford University class of 1950.

Sandra studied economics at the university. However, while she was at school, a legal problem with the ranch sparked her interest in law. She decided to go to law school. She felt lucky when Stanford Law School accepted her. For every one woman in her class, there were thirty men. At that time it was unusual for women to study for a career. She was able to combine her first year of law school with her last year of college, which is even more unusual.

In her second year of law school at Stanford, Sandra was working on the *Stanford Law Review*—a magazine published by law students about the law—when she met a very interesting young man. His name was John Jay O'Connor. For the next six weeks, Sandra and John went out together every night. It was hardly a surprise when Sandra invited John home to the ranch to meet her parents. John, a city boy, found the ranch to be a whole different world, but he tried hard to fit in. Sandra's father commented, "I've seen better cowboys," but he and Ada Mae liked John very much and were thrilled when John asked Sandra to marry him.

Sandra Day and John O'Connor were married at the Lazy B on December 20, 1952, six months after her graduation from law school. It was the start of an excit-

Sandra Day and John O'Connor happily cut the cake together during their wedding reception at the Lazy B ranch in 1952.

ing time for the young couple. Both looked forward to beginning to practice law and to starting a family. While John finished his last semester of law school, Sandra looked for a job near the school. Much to her surprise, she could not find a job as a lawyer. In the 1950s most firms did not want to hire women as lawyers. She thought one firm might want to hire her, but then the employer asked her how fast she could type. The company wanted to hire her as a secretary, a more traditional job for women. Sandra now looks back at that job search with amusement. "I was shocked," she says. "I think I was naive. I had never stopped to think that it might be hard to get a job."

When John graduated from Stanford Law School in 1953, he was posted in Germany as a lawyer for the United States Army. The couple saw the job as a challenge and an opportunity to get some experience in law and to travel in Europe. They did both! While John worked for the Army, Sandra found a job as a lawyer for the Quartermaster Corps, which bought food and other necessary items for the Army. On breaks, they visited fourteen countries and skied for several months in Austria. In all, they stayed in Europe for three exciting and memorable years. Then they came home to Arizona, and life quickly changed greatly.

First, John and Sandra studied for the Arizona bar exam. The bar exam is a long test that people who want to be lawyers must pass. Although it is a very difficult

> **Justice O'Connor has two high schools named for her—one in Texas and one in Arizona.**

test, Sandra and John both passed it on the first try. John soon began working for a law firm in Phoenix. Sandra, though, took on a new job: that of a mother. On October 8, 1957, John and Sandra welcomed their first son, Scott Hampton O'Connor.

Sandra immediately went about seeing how she could combine motherhood with a law career. Because she knew that the big law firms didn't even want to hire women, much less women who worked part-time, she decided to start her own law firm with a friend. She worked in the office in the mornings and then spent the rest of each day caring for Scott. Sandra remembers those as very happy days; she had always wanted to be a mother, and she had a wonderful son. She was also learning the law and loving it, helping people with all kinds of legal problems.

As Sandra's law practice grew, so too did her family. In 1960, her second son, Brian, was born. In 1962, she gave birth to a third son, Jay. Always a practical person, Sandra saw that it would be difficult to continue working while her boys were so small. She therefore decided to stay at home for a few years and to continue law practice at a later time.

Sandra's three sons kept her busy. As children do, the boys sometimes got into some innocent trouble, scrapes that worried the young mother at the time but

Sandra manages to get her three mischievous young sons to sit still for a moment in order to snap a picture.

about which she would later laugh. When the oldest son, Scott, was two or three, Sandra heard him laughing aloud one day and went to investigate. Much to her horror, she found him flushing a kitten down the toilet. Sandra was able to rescue the scared kitten. She then explained to Scott that animals deserved gentleness and respect, and nothing like that ever happened again.

One morning, two-year-old Brian wandered off while still in his pajamas. Sandra could not find him anywhere. Neighbors helped her look, and finally the sheriff's office got involved in the search. Some hours later, the searchers found him along the Arizona canal in the company of an old man who lived in a tar-paper shed there. Brian was just fine.

Jay followed in the footsteps of his mischievous brothers. When he was two, Sandra was cooking a casserole in the oven. Jay managed to open the hot oven and put cans of tomato sauce from the pantry inside. An hour or so later, the cans exploded, pushing the oven door open and splattering tomato sauce all over the kitchen. The cleaning lady who was at the house at the time thought it was blood and quit on the spot.

Justice O'Connor enjoys learning languages. She speaks a fair amount of Spanish and has also studied German and French.

Despite these funny (and sometimes slightly scary) incidents, Sandra, John, and the boys lived a very normal family life.

When Jay turned three and the other two boys were in school, Sandra decided to return to work part-time. Sandra was pleased when the Arizona attorney general offered her a job as a lawyer in his office. She would

When Sandra became an Arizona state senator,
there was only one other woman in the Senate.

work there for several years, increasing her hours each year until she was again working full-time. During these years, Sandra became more and more involved in politics, and always found time to volunteer for political causes. She enjoyed serving her community through public service.

In 1969, Sandra's service was recognized in an important way: The Arizona Republican party asked her to fill an empty seat in the Arizona Senate. She became one of only two women in the Senate at the time, but her fellow senators recognized her as a very capable colleague and praised her dedication and hard work. She was elected to a full term in 1972.

Then, in 1973, the Republican party needed to pick a new leader. The senators talked for a long time about who the best person for the job would be. Sandra was surprised but happy when her colleagues asked her to be their leader. While she was still a senator, Sandra now had an additional job: that of majority leader of the Arizona senate. She was the first woman to serve as majority leader of any state senate in the United States.

Sandra enjoyed politics, but after she completed her second full term as a senator, she decided to look for ways to return to the law. She was ready for new challenges.

Sandra decided to run for election as a judge. Because she was familiar to the voters, and popular, she easily won the election and took her seat as a trial court judge. This is a judge who listens and guides trials about crimes and contracts and other legal matters. She was a fair but demanding judge. Lawyers who tried cases in her courtroom knew that they must be prepared and do a good job. If they were, they got along with Judge O'Connor just fine. If they weren't, watch out! The new judge did not like to have her time wasted.

As a judge, Sandra began a judicial tradition that she follows to this day. She listened to each case and tried to understand the law and the facts of each. Even in cases where she had a personal opinion, she did not allow her own feelings to influence her judgment. The word "justice" to her meant fairness, and Sandra used the law to try to make sure that every person who came to her court found justice.

Her fairness and ability were noted by other lawyers in Arizona. Those who remembered her success as a senator encouraged her to run for governor of Arizona. But Sandra had had enough of politics, and

In June 2002, Justice O'Connor was inducted into the Cowgirl Hall of Fame in Fort Worth, Texas.

the job held no appeal. Another job did, though: the new governor gave her a promotion! Sandra Day O'Connor was now a judge on the Arizona Court of Appeals.

An appeals court is different from a trial court, because the judges do not preside over trials. Instead, they review cases that trial court judges have already decided. They usually work in teams of three with other appeals court judges to see whether the trial court judges came to the right decision. For eighteen months she reviewed cases and strengthened her skills as a judge. The work was rigorous and challenging, and Sandra loved it. She thought that this would be her job for life.

But it would only last for eighteen months. In 1981, Sandra read with interest that Potter Stewart was retiring from his position as an associate justice on the United States Supreme Court. She wondered whom President Reagan would appoint to replace Justice Stewart. As a judge, Sandra was influenced by the decisions of our nation's highest court. As a lawyer, she was naturally interested in the legal decisions the court made. Soon after their marriage, she and John had even visited the court. Because it was a Saturday, they could not go in, but John had posed on the steps of the court in his army uniform, and Sandra had taken his photo. That, she would later say, "was the closest I ever thought I would come to the Supreme Court."

In Washington, however, advisers to President Ronald Reagan had a different idea. The new president had promised during his campaign that he would appoint a woman to the Supreme Court. Now his team looked for a qualified woman to fill Stewart's job. Little did Sandra O'Connor know that she was high on their list of possible candidates. She thought that she was just an ordinary appeals court judge, living in the desert, far from the bustling city of Washington.

She was astonished to receive a phone call from the White House one day in July. Would she come to the White House to meet President Reagan? "Well, yes," she thought. It would be an adventure! She met with the president and found him easy to talk to. On her way home, she thought, "Well, that was fun, but thank goodness I won't have to do that job!" She did not think that there was any chance that the president would choose her to be the next justice, but she was grateful to have been considered.

A few days later, she was working in her chambers—another name for a judge's office—when her secretary interrupted her, saying, "The president is on the

Sandra meets with President Ronald Reagan in July 1981, when she was being considered as a nominee for the United States Supreme Court.

phone!" Sandra paused, took a deep breath, and pressed the button on her phone that would connect her to the president. "Would you accept my nomination to be the next Supreme Court justice?" he asked. In her nervousness and surprise, Sandra did not remember the details of the conversation, but she did say "Yes!" She would later learn that the president had been so impressed with her during their meeting that he had never even interviewed any other candidate for the job.

On July 7, 1981, President Reagan publicly announced his nomination for Potter Stewart's vacant seat on the Supreme Court: Sandra Day O'Connor, Arizona appeals court judge. "Who is this woman?" everyone wondered. Newspaper, radio, and television people swarmed around Phoenix to learn more about her. Sandra, though, was concentrating on her confirmation.

When the president nominates a candidate for the Supreme Court, the United States Senate must vote on whether the president's choice would be a good justice. To learn more about the candidate, the Senate holds hearings. The senators asked Sandra about her views on various topics and about her experience in the law. Sandra's confirmation hearings lasted several days. The senators asked her many difficult questions, but she tried to answer them all honestly and completely. She

Sandra had to testify about her political views and experience before the Senate Judiciary Committee at the hearing to confirm her selection as the first female justice of the Supreme Court.

must have done a good job, because, in the end, the Senate voted 99–1 to confirm her as a justice.

Sandra Day O'Connor was sworn in as the 102nd member of the United States Supreme Court on September 25, 1981. After the ceremony, she posed for photos with the chief justice, the president, and her family. Then she began work! On September 28, just a few days before the new Supreme Court term would begin, Sandra Day O'Connor entered her new chambers at the Supreme Court to start her job as an associate justice.

Sandra gathers with her family and Chief Justice Warren Burger in front of the U.S. Supreme Court before she is sworn in. From left to right are: her father Harry, her husband John, her mother Ada Mae, Sandra, Chief Justice Warren Burger, and her sons, Brian, Jay, and Scott.

Those first days would be much like the ones to follow over the next two decades. Together with the other eight justices on the court, Justice O'Connor would decide whether the lower courts had correctly decided cases. To do so, she would research the law and study the facts of the cases before her. She would also have to decide which cases she would review. The Supreme Court receives thousands of requests for review every year. However, the court can only look at about a hundred of them. One important job for a justice, therefore, is to choose cases for review that will have an impact on the country as a whole. The Supreme Court typically reviews cases dealing with the Constitution and with the way federal laws are interpreted.

To choose and decide cases, Justice O'Connor needs lots of help. Like the other justices, she has four law clerks, young lawyers for whom working for the justice for one year is a great honor. These clerks research the law and look over the petitions for review. Then they make recommendations to the justice about how the court should decide. Justice O'Connor also has two secretaries and a messenger, all of whom have worked for her for many years. Finally, the Supreme Court itself has about 300 employees from cafeteria workers to curators to police officers, all of whom are there to support the nine justices and to make sure that the court runs smoothly.

*The nine justices of the Supreme Court, including the
newly sworn-in Associate Justice Sandra Day O'Connor
in the conference room of the Supreme Court in 1981.*

From left to right: Harry A. Blackmun, Thurgood Marshall,
William J. Brennan, Warren Burger, Sandra Day O'Connor, Byron
White, Lewis Powell, William Rehnquist, and John Paul Stevens.

On a typical day, Justice O'Connor will meet with her clerks on cases up for review. Then she attends oral argument, where she and the other justices listen to lawyers explain why the lower courts did or did not decide a case correctly. During oral argument, Justice O'Connor asks the lawyers questions to help her understand the case better. Oral argument lasts about two hours on most mornings.

After oral argument, Justice O'Connor usually has lunch with the other justices in their private dining room. A few days each month, the justices meet in a conference room to talk about how to decide cases. They hold a secret discussion in which they vote on each case. No one but the justices is allowed in the conference room while the meeting takes place.

For the rest of the day, Justice O'Connor works on reading and writing opinions. The written decisions of the court on cases are called opinions. In an opinion, the members of the court explain the law and their decision in a particular case. Opinions can be as short as a few sentences or as long as a hundred pages or more. Because Justice O'Connor

Justice O'Connor enjoys listening to music of various kinds, including classical, Dixieland, bluegrass, and dance music.

The private dining room where the justices enjoy lunch together. Below: The conference room in the Supreme Court where the justices hold their confidential meetings

spends so much of her time reading the law and writing opinions, she has often said that reading and writing are really her primary job. Each year, or "term," as a Supreme Court year is called, Justice O'Connor writes twenty opinions or more. In some, she explains why she agrees with the majority of the court. This type of opinion is called a "majority opinion." In others, she disagrees with the majority. This type of opinion is called a "dissent."

Finally, the justice is often asked to give speeches. In a typical month, she gives several speeches across the country. The justice enjoys speaking, and she is very pleased to be asked, but she feels that her primary responsibility is at the court. Because she is asked to attend so many events and give so many speeches, she can only choose a few from the many requests.

Justice O'Connor enjoys her job a great deal. She is very friendly with the other eight justices and has enormous respect for them; she also likes her law clerks and office staff. However, she is sometimes discouraged by the fact that there is always too much to do. She wants to make sure that she can treat every case seriously and fairly, and reach a correct decision. To do so, she often must work long hours and ask her staff to work late with her.

Justice O'Connor's favorite book is a biography of John Adams, the second president of the United States.

Reaching a fair decision can be a hard thing to do. When she was a trial court judge in Arizona, Justice O'Connor once had to sentence a young mother to jail for writing bad checks, even knowing that the woman would not be able to see her children while she served her sentence. Although she told

A Great Boss

Justice O'Connor really appreciates the people who work for her. She knows that they share her goals of doing justice and making sure that the Constitution and laws are interpreted and enforced fairly. Therefore, she tries hard to treat her coworkers well. Justice O'Connor often cooks Tex-Mex or Southwestern food and brings it to the court on Saturdays for the law clerks who are working. She invites her law clerks to her home for Thanksgiving dinner. She bakes birthday cakes for her employees' birthdays and encourages everyone to take a break for a small party. She even organizes trips in the Washington area for her staff. In recent years, her employees have joined her on rafting, sightseeing, and hiking trips.

Justice O'Connor is also always concerned that her staff is safe and happy. One time, one of her clerks had to work late at night to finish an opinion. Justice O'Connor wanted to make sure that he could walk home safely. She therefore asked the Supreme Court police force to allow him to bring his dog into the court building so that he would have "company" walking home.

At the end of each Supreme Court term, Justice O'Connor makes a point of thanking each member of her staff for his or her hard work over the previous nine months. She knows that she could not do her job without them!

Supreme Court justices are often requested to speak at events across the country because their knowledge and experience are highly valued as a crucial part of the American legal system. Here, Justice O'Connor speaks to college students at Utah's Brigham Young University in 2002.

the young woman of her punishment with a straight face, she then went back into her chambers and cried.

When Justice O'Connor hears cases about children and families at the Supreme Court, it is also hard to reach a fair decision. However, her job is to make sure that everyone coming to the Supreme Court gets justice, and she decides each case based on what the law says, not on how she feels about it personally.

In one case, the parents of a disabled girl named Shannon Carter filed a lawsuit against her school. Shannon's parents claimed that the school district did not provide Shannon with a free and appropriate public education, as the law required. They said that the school knew Shannon was learning-disabled and did not prepare a suitable individualized education program for their daughter. As a result, Mr. and Mrs. Carter decided to send Shannon to a special private school for children who had learning disabilities. Her parents asked the school district for money to pay for Shannon's tuition at the private school. In this case, Justice O'Connor agreed with Shannon's parents that the school district should pay for Shannon's schooling. In her opinion, she wrote that the school district must give Mr. and Mrs. Carter the money.

In another case grandparents of two young children asked the Supreme Court to tell the children's mother to allow them to spend more time with their grandchildren. Even though Justice O'Connor is a grandmother who loves to spend time with her own grandchildren, she wrote that forcing a mother to make her children see their grandparents is wrong. Such a decision would intrude on a mother's right to make decisions about what is best for her children.

Justice O'Connor has always enjoyed athletics. She roots for Stanford's various teams and for the 2001 baseball world champion Arizona Diamondbacks.

In the summer of 1988, Justice O'Connor received some terrible news. Doctors told her that she had breast cancer, a very common form of cancer for women. Although she was frightened at the thought that she had a serious illness, the fifty-eight-year-old justice decided to treat the cancer as just another challenge or obstacle. Luckily, although doctors found a tumor, they were able to remove it. She said later that she had to keep herself busy to keep her mind off her illness.

Sandra and John O'Connor decorate their Christmas trees with models of Washington monuments and buildings and with small American flags.

In 2002, Sandra and John O'Connor celebrated their fiftieth wedding anniversary with a family trip to Ireland. Justice O'Connor is very proud of the fact that she has had a long, successful marriage and is very close to her family.

Today, at age seventy-two, Sandra Day O'Connor remains an active and enthusiastic mother, grandmother, and justice. She enjoys fly-fishing, tennis, golf, and outdoor activities of all kinds. She entertains frequently and makes dinner for her friends. She plays a mean game of bridge! She also loves to travel with her husband to interesting places. Recently, the O'Connors visited remote parts of

Justice O'Connor dances with her husband John at a ball in Washington, D.C. Their loving marriage has lasted over fifty years.

Now in her seventies, Justice O'Connor is still very active in her personal and professional life. Here, she breaks ground for a new academic building at New York University Law School.

Mongolia, a place they found fascinating. She has enjoyed winter skiing in Austria, seeing the mountain gorillas in the Mountains of the Moon in Africa, and fishing in Alaska.

Some people think that the justice will retire soon. Others say that she will become chief justice when the current chief, William Rehnquist, retires. She's even been mentioned as a possible vice-presidential candidate from time to time! Justice O'Connor scoffs at all of these rumors. For now, she says, she'll concentrate on being the best Supreme Court justice she knows how to be.

After all, who can think of a more important job?

■

Thanks in part to Justice O'Connor, the Supreme Court Justices at the beginning of the twenty-first century are more diverse than when she was first appointed. From left to right in the back row are: Ruth Bader Ginsberg, David Hackett Souter, Clarence Thomas, and Stephen Breyer; front row: Antonin Scalia, John Paul Stevens, William Rehnquist, Sandra Day O'Connor, and Anthony M. Kennedy.

Timeline

March 26, 1930: Sandra Day born in El Paso, Texas

1942: Graduates from Radford School for Girls

1946: Graduates from high school

June 1950: Graduates from Stanford with B.A. in economics

June 1952: Graduates from Stanford Law School

December 20, 1952: Marries John O'Connor on family ranch in Arizona

1953: Works as lawyer for Quartermaster Corps in Germany

1957: Passes Arizona bar exam

1957: First son, Scott, born

1960: Second son, Brian, born

1962: Third son, Jay, born

1965: Returns to work as assistant state attorney general

1969: Becomes Arizona state senator

Timeline continued

1973: Becomes first woman majority leader of the Arizona Senate

1974: Becomes Maricopa County superior court judge

1978: Declines Republican party urging to run for governor

1979: Becomes judge on Arizona Court of Appeals

1981: President Ronald Reagan announces nomination of Sandra Day O'Connor to fill Potter Stewart's empty seat on the U.S. Supreme Court

1981: Sworn in to serve as an associate justice on the United States Supreme Court

1988: Diagnosed with breast cancer

1989: Becomes grandmother with birth of Courtney Day O'Connor to son Scott and his wife, Joanie

2002: Inducted into the Cowgirl Hall of Fame

Sources

—■—

Author interview, Sandra Day O'Connor, November 1998.

_____ , Sandra Day O'Connor, October, 2001.

Biskupic, Joan. "Chief Justice O'Connor? 'Nonsense,' she says," *Chicago Sun-Times*, January 27, 2002.

Conversation, Supreme Court Public Information Office, July 1, 2002.

"Cowgirl O'Connor," *The Philadelphia Inquirer*, June 10, 2002.

Florence County School District v. *Carter*, 114 S.Ct. 361 (1993).

Greenhouse, Linda. "Happy Trails," *New York Times*, February 3, 2002.

Interview with Sandra Day O'Connor, "Dateline NBC & Katie Couric," February 2002.

Interview with Sandra Day O'Connor, "Newshour with Jim Lehrer," February 1, 2002, www.pbs.org/newshour/bb/entertainment/jan-june02/oconnor_2-1.html.

Letter, Sandra Day O'Connor to author, November 23, 2001.

O'Connor, Sandra Day, and H. Alan Day. *Lazy B: Growing Up on a Cattle Ranch in the American Southwest*, New York: Random House, Inc., 2002.

"Oyez, Oyez, Oyez: Sandra Day O'Connor," www.oyez.nwu.edu/
justices.

Rosen, Jeffrey. "The O'Connor Court: America's Most Powerful
Jurist," *The New York Times Magazine*, June 3, 2001.

Speech by Sandra Day O'Connor, Boston, March 18, 1998.

Troxel v. *Granville*, 120 S.Ct. 2054 (2000).

Wood, Sean. "Cowgirl Hall to Induct Justice Sandra Day O'Connor,"
Fort Worth Star-Telegram, April 30, 2002.

www.supremecourtus.gov (official Web site of the United States
Supreme Court)

Index

Page numbers in *italics* refer to illustrations